Piano/Vocal/Guitar

Southern Gospel Classics

Page	Title
2	Been Through Enough
7	Born to Serve the Lord
10	Daddy Sang Bass
13	Faith Unlocks the Door
16	Fall to Fly
21	Give Up
24	Goodby, World, Goodby
32	He Came Looking for Me
27	Honestly
38	I Can't Help Myself
44	I Saw the Light
47	I Wouldn't Take Nothing for My Journey Now
50	I'm Gonna Sing
53	It Is No Secret (What God Can Do)
56	Look for Me (Around the Throne)
73	More Like a Whisper
66	New Born Man
70	One More Valley
78	The Promise
90	Sacrifice of Praise
87	Sheltered in the Arms of God
96	Show Me the Way to Go
102	Ten Thousand Angels
110	That's When the Angels Rejoice
107	The Three Nails
116	Through the Fire
124	'Til the Storm Passes By
134	Wait for the Light to Shine
127	The Walk
138	What a Day That Will Be
141	Your First Day in Heaven

ISBN 978-1-4234-8791-3

HAL•LEONARD® CORPORATION

7777 W. BLUEMOUND RD. P.O. BOX 13819 MILWAUKEE, WI 53213

For all works contained herein:
Unauthorized copying, arranging, adapting, recording, Internet posting, public performance, or other distribution of the printed music in this publication is an infringement of copyright.
Infringers are liable under the law.

Visit Hal Leonard Online at
www.halleonard.com

BEEN THROUGH ENOUGH

Words and Music by
CONSTANT CHANGE

DADDY SANG BASS

Words and Music by
CARL PERKINS

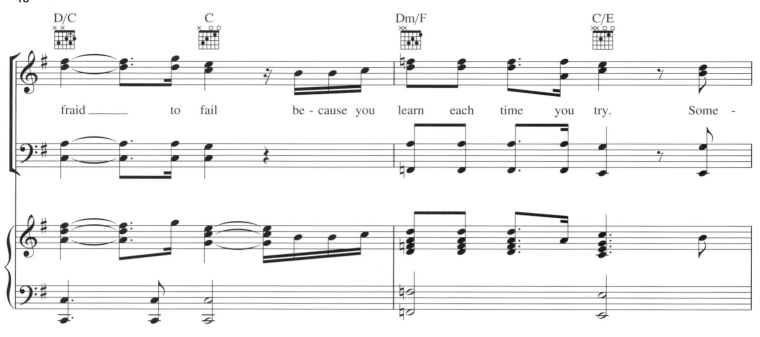
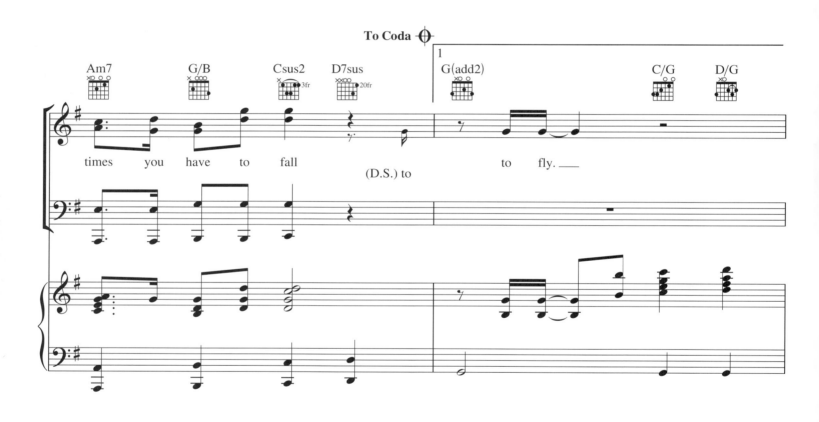
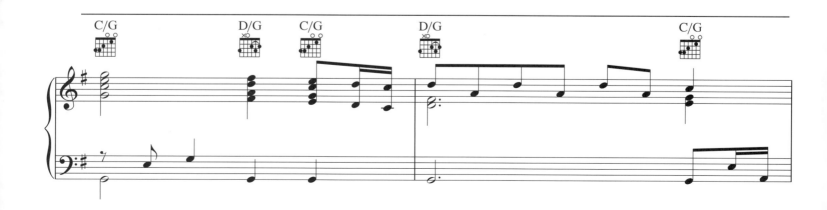

GIVE UP

Words and Music by
HOWARD GOODMAN

Slow Gospel feel, in 4

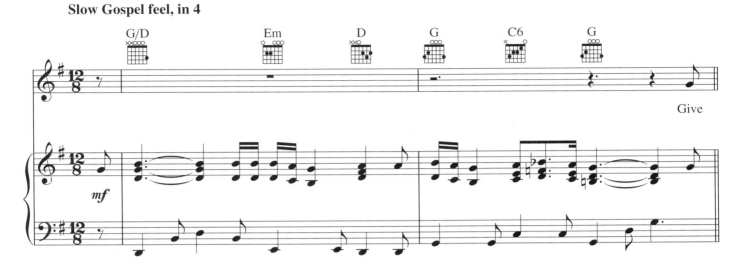

up____ and let Je-sus take o - ver.____ Give

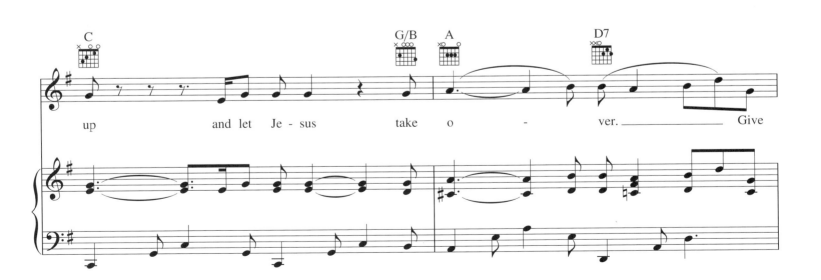

up____ and let Je-sus take o - ver.____ Give

Copyright © 1957 UNIVERSAL - CEDARWOOD PUBLISHING
Copyright Renewed
All Rights Reserved Used by Permission

HONESTLY

I CAN'T HELP MYSELF

Words and Music by GRANT CUNNINGHAM and MATT HUESMANN

© 2003 MEADOWGREEN MUSIC COMPANY (ASCAP), IMAGINE THE MUSIC (ASCAP) and MATT HUESMANN MUSIC (ASCAP)
MEADOWGREEN MUSIC COMPANY and IMAGINE THE MUSIC Admin. by EMI CMG PUBLISHING
MATT HUESMANN MUSIC Admin. by BUG MUSIC
All Rights Reserved   Used by Permission

I SAW THE LIGHT

Words and Music by
HANK WILLIAMS

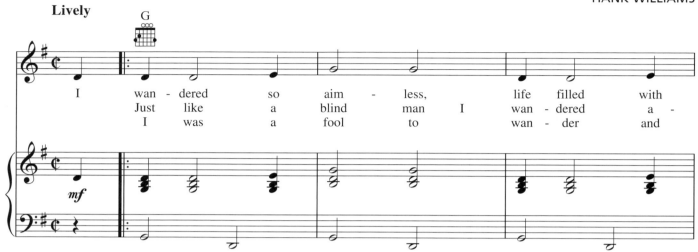
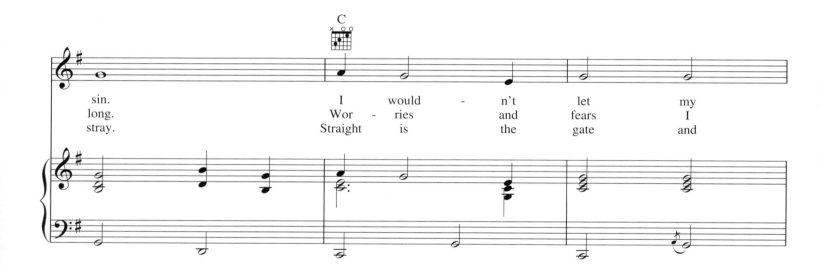

Copyright © 1948 Sony/ATV Music Publishing LLC and Hiriam Music in the U.S.A.
Copyright Renewed
All Rights on behalf of Hiriam Music Administered by Rightsong Music Inc.
All Rights outside the U.S.A. Administered by Sony/ATV Music Publishing LLC
All Rights on behalf of Sony/ATV Music Publishing LLC Administered by Sony/ATV Music Publishing LLC, 8 Music Square West, Nashville, TN 37203
International Copyright Secured   All Rights Reserved

I WOULDN'T TAKE NOTHING FOR MY JOURNEY NOW

Words and Music by JIMMIE DAVIS
and CHARLES F. GOODMAN

IT IS NO SECRET
(What God Can Do)

Words and Music by
STUART HAMBLEN

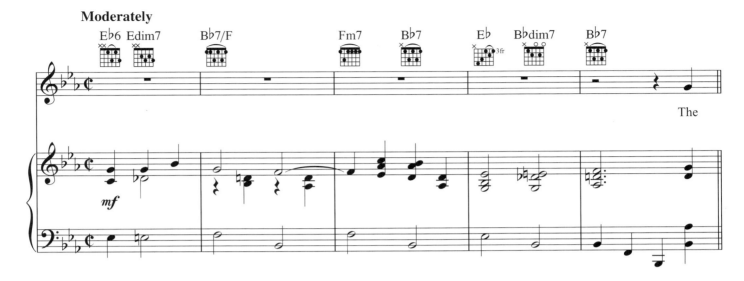
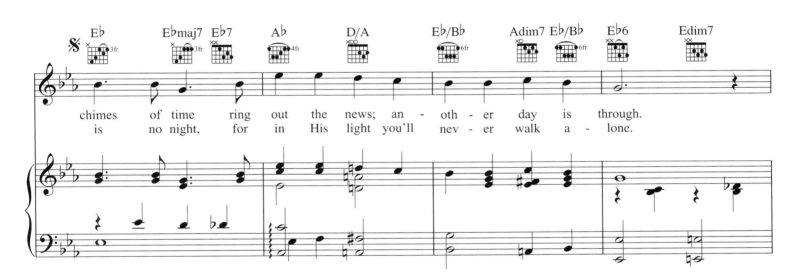
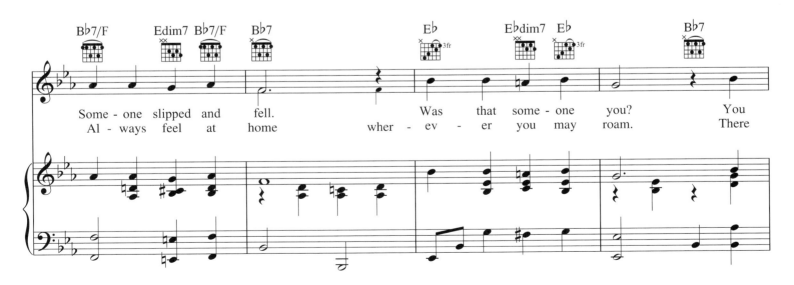

Copyright © 1950 SONGS OF UNIVERSAL, INC.
Copyright Renewed
All Rights Reserved   Used by Permission

LOOK FOR ME
(Around the Throne)

Words and Music by LANDY EWING,
GERON DAVIS and TIME PEDIGO

© 1988 MEADOWGREEN MUSIC COMPANY (ASCAP)
Admin. by EMI CMG PUBLISHING
All Rights Reserved   Used by Permission

NEW BORN MAN

Words and Music by
JOHN R. CASH

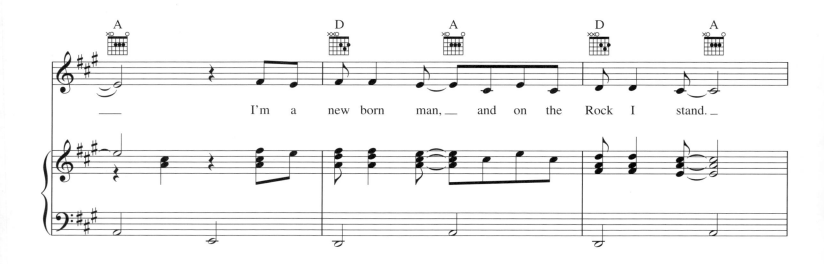
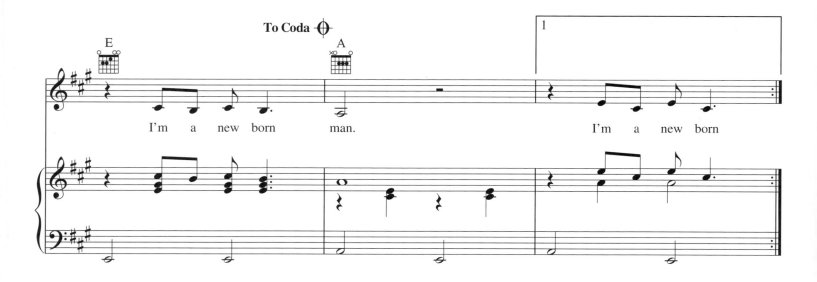

© 1976 (Renewed 2004) SONG OF CASH, INC. (ASCAP)/Administered by BUG MUSIC
All Rights Reserved   Used by Permission

THE PROMISE

Words and Music by DONALD POYTHRESS
and BRIAN WHITE

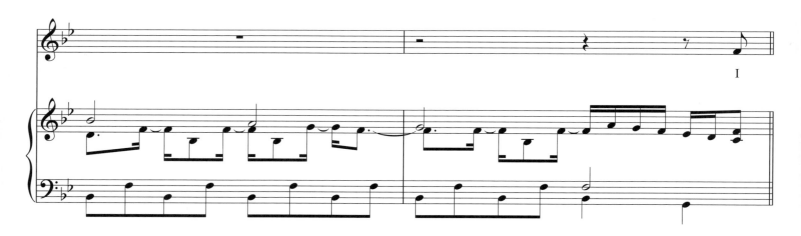

Copyright © 2002 by Universal Music - MGB Songs and Multisongs, Inc.
International Copyright Secured   All Rights Reserved

SACRIFICE OF PRAISE

Words and Music by
GERALD CRABB

SHOW ME THE WAY TO GO

Words and Music by
JEFF TWEEL

Copyright © 1987 Sony/ATV Music Publishing LLC
All Rights Administered by Sony/ATV Music Publishing LLC, 8 Music Square West, Nashville, TN 37203
International Copyright Secured   All Rights Reserved

98

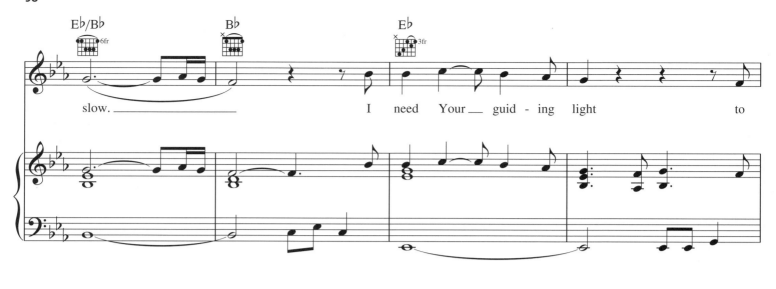
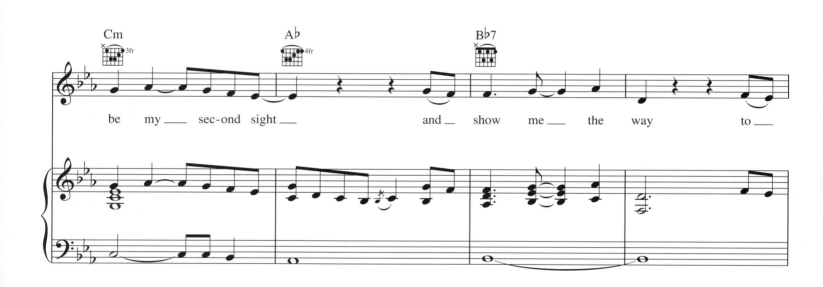

TEN THOUSAND ANGELS

Words and Music by
RAY OVERHOLT

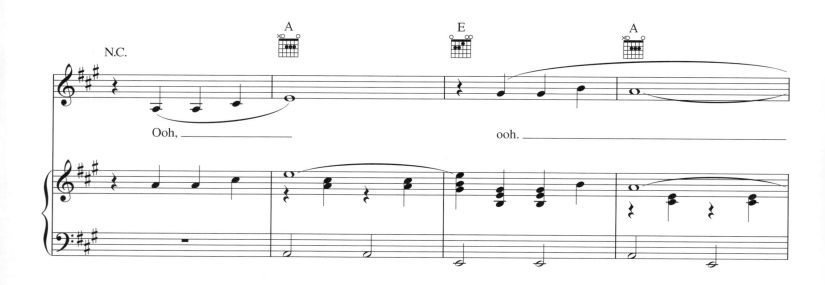

© 1959 (Renewed) PSALMSINGER MUSIC (Administered by THE COPYRIGHT COMPANY, Nashville, TN)
All Rights Reserved   International Copyright Secured   Used by Permission

107

THE THREE NAILS

Words and Music by
JIMMIE DAVIS

Copyright © 1970 Peermusic Ltd.
Copyright Renewed
International Copyright Secured   All Rights Reserved

THAT'S WHEN THE ANGELS REJOICE

Words and Music by
LARRY BRYANT

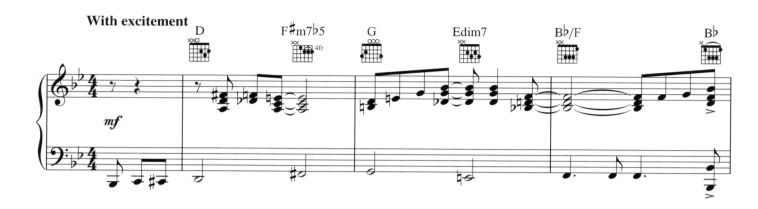

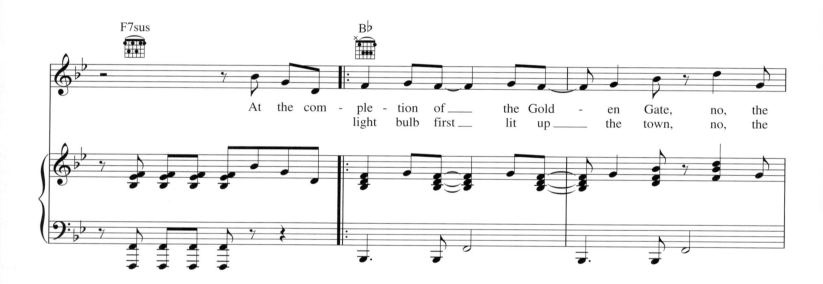

At the com-ple-tion of the Gold-en Gate, no, the
light bulb first lit up the town, no, the

an-gels did not cel-e-brate. And when the Wright boys flew their bird,
an-gels did not dance a-round. And when the man stepped on the moon,

© 1983 STONEBROOK MUSIC COMPANY (SESAC)
Admin. by EMI CMG PUBLISHING
All Rights Reserved Used by Permission

THE WALK

Words and Music by
GERALD CRABB

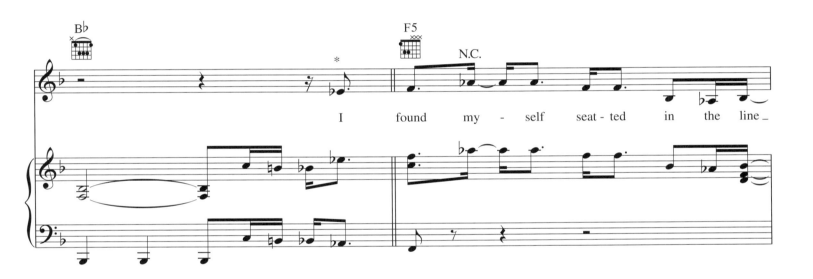

*Male vocal written at pitch.

Copyright © 2003 MPCA Lehsem Songs, Christian Taylor Music and Daywind Music Publishing
MPCA Lehsem Songs Administered by MPCA Music, LLC
International Copyright Secured All Rights Reserved

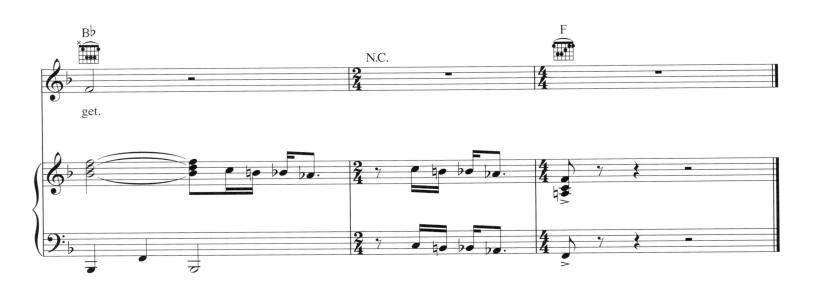

WAIT FOR THE LIGHT TO SHINE

Words and Music by
FRED ROSE

Copyright © 1943 Sony/ATV Music Publishing LLC
Copyright Renewed
All Rights Administered by Sony/ATV Music Publishing LLC, 8 Music Square West, Nashville, TN 37203
International Copyright Secured   All Rights Reserved

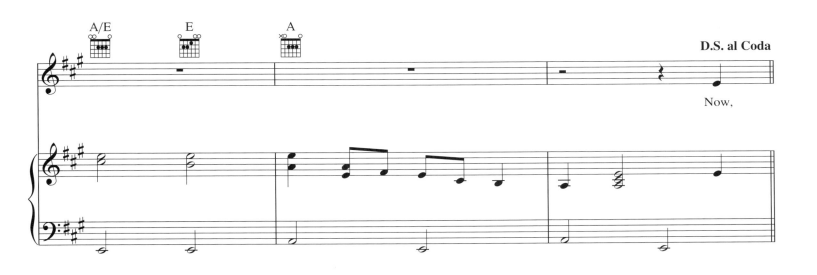
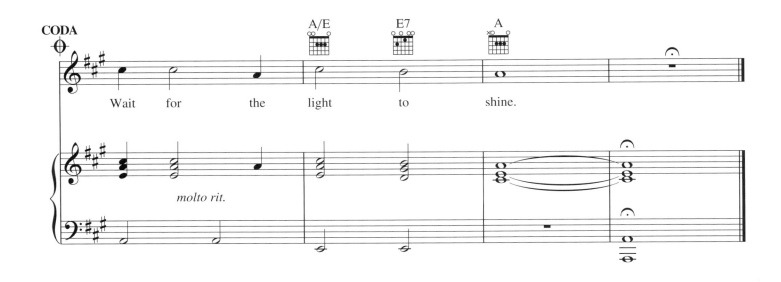

YOUR FIRST DAY IN HEAVEN

Words and Music by
STUART HAMBLEN

THE BEST EVER COLLECTION
ARRANGED FOR PIANO, VOICE AND GUITAR

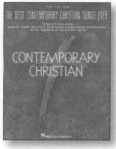     

150 of the Most Beautiful Songs Ever
150 ballads
00360735 .... $24.95

150 More of the Most Beautiful Songs Ever
150 songs
00311318 .... $24.95

Best Acoustic Rock Songs Ever
65 acoustic hits
00310984 .... $19.95

Best Big Band Songs Ever
68 big band hits
00359129 .... $16.95

Best Broadway Songs Ever
83 songs
00309155 .... $24.95

More of the Best Broadway Songs Ever
82 songs
00311501 .... $22.95

Best Children's Songs Ever
102 tunes
00310360 (Easy Piano) $19.95

Best Christmas Songs Ever
69 holiday favorites
00359130 .... $19.95

Best Classic Rock Songs Ever
64 hits
00310800 .... $19.99

Best Classical Music Ever
86 classical favorites
00310674 (Piano Solo) $19.95

Best Contemporary Christian Songs Ever
50 favorites
00310558 .... $19.95

Best Country Songs Ever
78 classic country hits
00359135 .... $19.95

Best Early Rock 'n' Roll Songs Ever
74 songs
00310816 .... $19.95

Best Easy Listening Songs Ever
75 mellow favorites
00359193 .... $19.95

Best Gospel Songs Ever
80 gospel songs
00310503 .... $19.95

Best Hymns Ever
118 hymns
00310774 .... $18.95

Best Jazz Standards Ever
77 jazz hits
00311641 .... $19.95

More of the Best Jazz Standards Ever
74 beloved jazz hits
00311023 .... $19.95

Best Latin Songs Ever
67 songs
00310355 .... $19.95

Best Love Songs Ever
65 favorite love songs
00359198 .... $19.95

Best Movie Songs Ever
74 songs
00310063 .... $19.95

Best Praise & Worship Songs Ever
80 all-time favorites
00311057 .... $19.95

More of the Best Praise & Worship Songs Ever
80 songs
00311800 .... $19.99

Best R&B Songs Ever
66 songs
00310184 .... $19.95

Best Rock Songs Ever
63 songs
00490424 .... $18.95

Best Songs Ever
72 must-own classics
00359224 .... $22.95

More of the Best Songs Ever
79 more favorites
00310437 .... $19.95

Best Soul Songs Ever
70 hits
00311427 .... $19.95

Best Standards Ever, Vol. 1 (A-L)
72 beautiful ballads
00359231 .... $17.95

More of the Best Standards Ever, Vol. 1 (A-L)
76 all-time favorites
00310813 .... $17.95

Best Standards Ever, Vol. 2 (M-Z)
72 songs
00359232 .... $17.95

More of the Best Standards Ever, Vol. 2 (M-Z)
75 stunning standards
00310814 .... $17.95

Best Torch Songs Ever
70 sad and sultry favorites
00311027 .... $19.95

Best TV Songs Ever
64 catchy theme songs
00311048 .... $17.95

Best Wedding Songs Ever
70 songs
00311096 .... $19.95

FOR MORE INFORMATION, SEE YOUR LOCAL MUSIC DEALER, OR WRITE TO:

7777 W. BLUEMOUND RD. P.O. BOX 13819 MILWAUKEE, WI 53213

Visit us on-line for complete songlists at
www.halleonard.com

Prices, contents and availability subject to change without notice. Not all products available outside the U.S.A.

0309